STUDENTS WITH PEN

ADVENTURE INTO POETRY

ASST. CABINET 2021-2022

Copyright © Asst. Cabinet 2021-2022
All Rights Reserved.

Contents

Contents

Contents

Acknowledgements

The world is improved by those who aspire to advance and inspire others. The best mentors are the ones that give their time as a gift to guide aspiring leaders. Everyone who strives to improve oneself and others are appreciated.

We have taken steps to ensure that this book is error-free in terms of grammar, spelling, and plagiarism. But without the generous efforts of the 9–12 students of GS, the direction of the English department, Sadiqa Taranum (HM), Vice Principal of GS Farhadunnisa (VP) and our cherished librarian Nabeela, none of this would have been possible.

Our gratitude goes out to Fatimath Hiba of 12A6, the author of Shine With Hopes: Be A Diamond & Miznah Gulfisha Ali of 12A5 for the wonderful illustration of the cover.

We are grateful to everyone who contributed freely and to the best of their skills.

1. Something Eternal

Love is an illusion,
it can be fiction,
At heart it causes destruction,
But real love is true
Where tears show honesty
Where the mind is constant
Where the heart beats for you
Where the happiness and hope are you
and THE LOVE for you is always real
That's why we say "love is beautiful" and "love is eternal"

- Jenna Najeeb - 9A9

2. Bees

Once I called a bee at my house to play games and pass time!
The bee was arrogant it denied my call and went on its way!
It went from flower to flower,
and then to its hive!
It just kept working the whole day,
And I kept pushing the buttons on the joystick to win the race!
Six weeks passed by and the bee had passed away by then!
Mom called me downstairs;
'Oh, son eat some honey!',
I went rushing down and ate the honey,
Thanked my mom for such a sweet treat and went to the sink,
The spoon had some honey still left but I was lazy to wipe it off
with my tongue and kept it as it was!
Mom called me down after seeing the spoon I left!
She told:
Oh, son! What have you done?
You've wasted the bee's hard work!
I told:
Oh, mom!
The bees are arrogant and won't indulge in playing games!
Why must I wipe off all the honey when that silly bee denied my
call?

Mom told:
Silly was you son!
A bee's life span,
six weeks long,
But it never passes the time!
A bee travels almost the distance equal to one globe!
A bee dies working hard!
While we humans die passing time!

– Mahin Ayesha Class – 9A5

3. This shall also Pass

Many of us are sad or depressed

But we don't realise that we are blessed

And that this life is just a test All you have to do is try your best

I am pretty sure that people always tell you this

But all of them we dismiss

Your thoughts are the main cause of this

The good in everything they seem to miss

What you don't realise is that your thoughts are control

And to fix this there is only one thing to do

That is to get closer to the one who created you

For he will help you change your point of view

With a pure soul, heart and mind

Everything will seem like a new kind

Another thing you need to see

If you want to talk about how you feel

Just look in a mirror

You are your best understander

If you find that a bit too odd

Remember you always have God

He is the best listener and knows about everything you've gone through

Have faith in him for he can ma ke your prayers come true.

Whatever he does is for your good It's okay if you misunderstood.
We all are facing our battles
Whether on the street or in castles.
But keep faith and positivity in front of you.
I'm sure what I say is true.

- Hafsah Abbasia Khan - 9A5

4. Unknown Depths

Listen to the waves crash,
how the pebble makes a splash.
The smallest factor can turn
into something huge in return
You don't know how deep the blue water is
like the problem you're getting yourself in.
You're on a boat that will sink,
perhaps it's time that you rethink.
Your choices, your decisions, are they right?
remember, in the deep end, there's no light
because once the tide attacks violently, stronger than before,
the ebbing tide will make it harder for you to swim back to the
shore.
I can see your mind going into a whirlpool,
but don't forget, the oyster reveals a pearl, a jewel.
I know the currents may be strong,
and there's a lot that can go wrong,
but just dive the tides,
don't worry, I'll be by your side.
I promise you won't drown again in the cimmerian gloom
where inevitably you're the fish the shark will consume
Gather the shells, and stroll down the seashore.

Do you feel much better than before?
After all, as they say, "dance with the waves, move with the sea
and let the rhythm of the water set your soul free.

- Yaseera Abid - 9A5

5. Days like these

Been waiting for this day for a while,
Where I start my day with a tender smile,
The breathtaking warmglow coloured swirls of the sunrise
ever so gently as sparkles fill my eyes
Hearing the dawn chorus from the trees,
As I feel the pleasant refreshing breeze
It's on mornings like these,
when I feel most at ease.
I'd honestly just lay on the grass,
and wish this time would never pass,
because I feel the comfort whenever
I gaze at clouds and enjoy the weather.
Humming soothing dulcet tones,
to myself when I'm alone,
These moments, filled with an abundance of bliss
When they're over, I know I'll reminisce.
These moments I would seize,
I stri ve for days like these.
If only, I could rewind and repeat,
But, without hardships, life is incomplete,
as both joy and woes make it bittersweet.

- Yaseera Abid - 9A5

• 9 •

6. Goal

Everyone has a goal in life,
But I couldn't decide mine
They tell me to move forward in this race of life
Feeling lonely I never knew I was behind.
I walked and walked
Looking for a destination
They thought so, but I was searching
For inspiration!
For a moment I thought
"do I have a certain role?
What is my individual goal?"
Then I realized,
Choices come and go
So do what you want to do
Don't lose yourself over
On something you don't think is right for you.
Follow your heart
Follow the lead
In the end, you will have a
Successful dream.

- Sobia Noorain - 9A7

7. The GOLDEN AGE

Whether it was hide and seek,
Or any other game,
Only contentment existed,
And no desire for fame.
The little pocket money which made me a Queen,
That scolding from mom on seeing a stubborn stain on my shirt,
That insecurity about seeing dad,
Pouring love to my little sister!
Those days were not a bed of roses,
Instead, they were roses with thorns.
Thorns of hurdles, pains, sadness and fear!!
I'm not yet an adult;
I am still a child.
A child who's enjoying her life.
A soul who dreams,
To become an Author!!

- Sheza Umar - 9A5

8. BATTLE BETWEEN MY THOUGHTS!

I have many thoughts in my head,
Well; none of them is said.
I'm afraid of what you'll think,
When I say that I flink,
You don't know how I feel,
What I show you aren't real.
You never see the signs,
And you think I am fine.
Because I've never said,
All the thought that's,
Alive inside my head!!

- Sheza Umar - 9A5

9. MY ROLE MODEL!

When I was a kid, she helped me become who I
am today, and taught me all I had to know.
From my babyhood till here,
Continuously working hard.
Those comforting sweet words which would heal away
my wounds!
She senses my problems, with no hesitation.
The one who picks me up whenever I fall,
She's my Google, she knows it all!
Concerned about me, care about me,
Always behind me for everything I need.
She's the sunlight of my day,
I feel blessed to have her by my side!!
O' Beautiful;
You might grow old in years,
But the youngest one in my pages.
She is my LOVE, my LIFE, my MOM!!!

- Sheza Umar - 9A5

10. TRY, TRY AND TRY UNTIL YOU ACHIEVE IT!

I'm trying,
But it always feels like I'm dying,
I want to persist,
But my mind insists.
I get scared,
But I never really cared,
I started achieving things,
And kept on running.
Ever Since;
Things were stunning!
Don't give up,
Try, Try and Try until you achieve it!!
You only live once,
So utilize it in the best way possible!!

- Sheza Umar - 9A5

11. Cliche

Like a memory it stays,
With time it fades.
Small steps we take,
And we know the stake.
Going through the memory lane,
We wish the time remained!
The world seemed tempting then,
Now we know the cage.
The sweet , salty and bitter taste,
The memory always fascinates!

- Wahiba Kaleem Alam - 10A7

12. Love Yourself

"Love yourself" - two words, much work
self-love and compassion.
Comparison and obsession
A great conflict, and which to choose?
I am neither - a given.
2 sides of a coin,
where one remains hidden
and the other a 'vision'.
leading me to an ending
Lies the versions of me pretending.
" Will I ever reach there? "
An ever-lasting war - residing in me.

- Gopikka - 10A9

13. Memories of Mine

As time passes by,
My life goes high.
Sometimes unhurriedly,
Sometimes rapidly.
No replays, no rewinds,
But when I see back,
I see my childhood.
Filled with happiness,
Filled with naughtiness,
A carefree life with no worries.
I see myself singing through the valleys,
I see myself dancing through the hills.
I remember being punished,
I remember being praised.
Thinking of all this makes me feel,
To be a child again.
If I would get a chance,
To wish for something true.
I could wish for intelligence or riches,
But I would wish for my,
Childhood to be back.

- Reshmi John - 10A7

14. Because she is a Girl

Once upon a time,
There was a friend of mine.
Who had a question in her mind,
For which the answer she wanted to find.
Why can't I go to school?
Why do I have special rules?
Why do people look down on me?
Why do they look with a frown on me?
Why am I not a pearl?
Is it because I'm a girl?
She's a daughter and a sister,
She's a friend and a mother.
She's a treasure which many don't realise,
And a blessing or a real prize.
She wants to be seen,
She wants to be known.
All she wants is freedom,
And nothing more.
Then she knew the truth,
Which was not her youth.
The answer was not tender,
Because it was her gender.

Yes, it was, because she's a girl.

- Reshmi John - 10A9

15. My First Love

He taught me to give a voice,

He taught me to stroll.

He gives me so much love,

That I expect nothing above.

He also gets sad,

He also gets mad,

He gets tired of me,

But still, he makes time for me.

He is someone indescribable,

With so much love.

People say he is a hero,

People say he is fun.

But I have a special name for him,

For me, he is my dad.

- Reshmi John - 10A7

16. Picture of the Day

The Morning today, is more special than ever,
In the soothing wind that rushed from the east, I went deep into
the happy memories.
The dew shook the mind and the soil
The memories of the shore that fell in love with the sea,
And The broken dreams
Allow wa ter to spread through you
The slow flow of it will help itself to spread, sometimes it grows,
bloom
Give away its smell
That what you want will be yours forever till the mountains are
high and the sky is blue
Then if you again pamper the plants it will rain on you like dew
drops,
The fresh air makes you feel special,
that day we will mix with nature,
No one will be there to defeat us other than rain by flood, and
wind by a wind storm.
Feel nature and admire the magic of love. happiness and peace.

- Swetha Shiju - 10A9

17. Street Life

Eyewatering steams and nose —whelming smells cloud this
tandoori,
all foods prepared here; sweet or savoury.
Over the clatter and chatter I ask simply, humbly — for a
splatter of a batter.
But am simply denied:
Go outside.
Of all places, I could sleep it was here,
across. Woken early by the fear
a passing car evoked on me, sirens wailing;
observe rich men smoke out on the balcony railing.
Once again I smell it all; mixed spices, tomato, garlic
freshly taunting me — I can have not one lick.

- Nuboogh Hassan - 10A8

18. Smile : A Veil

I thought
you were happy
and
your life was lazy
to make you gloomy,
I thought
you didn't know LIFE
and why people cry
as you always try
to make someone bright,
I thought
your life was
awesome and cheerful
just because
you always appeared to SMILE,
But I was wrong
terribly
wrong again;
I'm sorry
sorry,
I didn't know
you had your own life story

to tell as
tears burst from
your eyes,
I didn't know
you had smiled and laughed
all days with me to veil your
broken heart,
I didn't know
that people use
SMILE
as a veil like me,
At Least
now I have learned that
everyone who smiles
aren't happy,
At least now
I have learned
that
SMILE can be a veil for
broken hearts.

- Aysha Sheza - XA1

19. Thought for the Day

Our life is like a train.
At starting it has many passengers,
But then slowly they leave as their destination arrives.
Sometimes some of them leave before their destination
Wish we could stop them.
Wish we could change the route so that their destination never
arrives.
But the train can't run on the track forever.
Someday it has to stop.

- Ayesha Saad - XA3

20. The Call

Won't you open your eye,
And see me cry
Don't you feel my pain,
And notice the vain.
Just throw your arms,
And hold me tight
I love being your child,
If you were in sight
I would hope with delight.
Take me through the ways
The ones that weren't walked before,
Lead me through trails
You walked before
Ride me through dark,
Let's wonder in ease
Hold me through the path,
Let's not stumble and fall.
Don't rush me
through paradise,
Let me see it
once and for all.
Won't you open your eye,

And see me cry
Don't you feel my pain,
And notice the vain.
Maybe all this is an illusion,
Just a mere imagination
I know there is a mystery beyond,
Where my feet can aford.
Just let me know
if am I worthy of being your child.
Just let me know,
The meaning of life.

- Belva Biju- XA6

21. A New Home

A house built with rigid bricks and aching stones
But home is never built alone
With loving arms a mother takes
Her newborn in her hands
That is home
Far better than those built on land
It takes a lot to build a home
But a house is made in a day
You need to build with love
And fill emotions in walls of clay
Home is where we learn to grow
we learn to love
we have learned to let go
For it is built for a long time
That is why my home
Is very dear to mine.

- Sarah Ahmed - 10A9

22. Roar and leap and go for it, little blooming seeds

You are the seeds of the future, full of budding thoughts,
Your heart is pounding aloud with ideas of all sorts;
Yours thrive for learning will take you to new heights,
Don't get complacent, hold on but do fight for your rights.
Roar and leap and go for it, little blooming seeds......
Set your dreams high and keep your sights fixed on the goal,
Master each moment with focus and follow your inner soul;
Live in the present, let your hard work do its part,
Growth means how much you gave; not how much you have got.
Roar and leap and go for it, little blooming seeds......
You will learn important life lessons from each path you travel,
Listen to the voice of your h eart, be clear, all the mysteries of life
will unravel;
Don't count how many times you made mistakes, just learn from
them,
Be persistent, as long as you try, you will rise again and become a
gem.
Roar and leap and go for it, little blooming seeds.....
Apathy, Negativity and Pessimism will never let you be unique,

Ah! You have to win the weary battle; your wishes shouldn't be weak;
Stay Optimistic and remember the greatest failure is the failure to try,
But along the journey be Respectful, Empathetic and don't make anyone cry.
So, Roar and leap and go for it, little blooming seeds...

– Sawsan Jeelani – XA3

23. The Obsessed Artist

The canvas was white

when she saw it in the store

she painted it a beautiful colour

But now her fingers ache and sore

With every inching hour

That feel like seconds flying away

She spends her time, locked all-day

Her skin peels off like dried paint

As her lips lose colour and their youthful taint

She plays with paints

As musicians play the guitars

She glimpses into futures afar

She sees secrets unravel

Like a spool of thread

She knows her illness

Yet she paints in her bed

She is told to respite a million different times

close your eyes, rest a little while

It pains to see her vanishing away

She cries and wails

As her hair turns grey

If only we could see

The paintings she hides
If only we could know
Her genius inside
We all have an artist
Lost in years
Discover yours
For I have met mine

– Sarah Ahmed – 10A9

24. Oh Teacher!

Life's mysteries,
roads wouldn't have been discovered,
Oh, teacher! Had you not uncovered them with your patience for
us;
Expanding our knowledge and developing our skills,
Your endurance and forbearance help us to climb uphill;
You boost our morale and inspire us not to get disappointed,
No doubt life is tough, but it will for sure give us many chances;
You help us go through our trials and tribulations,
No wonder we call you the building blocks of the Nation;
Without your zeal and zest, so many things would have
remained unseen,
You make us walk upon the unwalked and put our feet where
they have
never been;
Whenever we need you, you're always there, knowing just
what to do,
Oh, teacher! Words could never explain how we feel about you...

- Sawsan Jeelani - XA3

25. Pandemic

The covid pandemic has changed our lives so much,
Now we all need a divine healing touch;
During these online classes,
New prescription and new glasses
Switching on the cameras became mandatory,
Staring at the screen became obligatory;
Waiting for the ID and passcode,
Oh! It's too much of an overload…
But always remember, after grief there is ease,
At least we all are safe from this deadly disease;
In all the quietness and peace around,
There is a special type of kindness that we all have found…
Remember, Gratefulness is the quality of righteousness,
We all must thank our teachers who hel ped us;
Promise! None of us will give up as the end of a pandemic is in
sight;
We will continue working together until we all win this
FIGHT…..

- Sawsan Jeelani - XA3

26. Crying Smiles

She lives down the street,
has too much time to keep,
Fills her home with lonely roses,
as she fills the heat of lonely neighbours.
she lives for the people,
While the thorny roses cut her,
As blood flows with tears,
She paints a smile with the bloody smears.

- Nada Najeeb Kalappadan - 11A1

27. Silenced Beauty

Many speak about what we must be,
Thousands believe they deserve to preach,
In the chaos of worldly opinions,
The voice supreme gets trodden.
Years of false saints,
have stolen lives great,
A soul genius and feminine,
Reduced to mere melanin.
Problems treated with indifference,
Rewarding heights of fear and silence,
Drowning the mighty blaze,
A radiance brighter than beauty.

- Nada Najeeb Kalappadan - 11A1

28. Love Thyself

If you lift thy sight,
Off the books of laws,
Lay thy sight,
In the world of flaws,
You shall see a beauty none tread,
Verses more heavenly left unread.
Mother nature rises far above,
A human soul could ever crawl,
So rest thy worries of the trolls,
And let nature take its stroll.
Feel the beauty beyond sight,
Bask in the glory of this heavenly might,
Never let your soul shatter,
Peace shall be brought to you on a golden platter.
Love thyself in war and peace,
Rest shall fall in place by ease.

- Nada Najeeb Kalappadan - 11A1

29. Despair

A hollow puncture in your thought process,
Blessings great feel insignificant to your heart's losses,
Fear of the unknown,
Saddened by the well-known.
Fuel to the soul seems to be dying,
Wakes up every day for a series of lying,
False hopes to feel brightened,
Brightened light diminishes the light of the lightened.
But truly again,
One hopes it gets better,
Better when let's leave it for the future to settle.
Mind games a thousand cannot play,
Binds the ones that do in dismay.

- Nada Najeeb Kalappadan - 11A1

30. Castle in the Air

If the sky is a success,
Then the balloon shall be my ride,
I shall fill it with hope,
And let my dreams take flight.
I shall float in the air,
My everlasting shrine,
If the sky is the limit,
Then the space shall be mine!
If the land keeps me away,
From my castle in the air,
I shall cloud my ears,
And take the fight anyway.
If the birds are my terrors and rains are my battles,
I shall fill a little more hope,
And float away!

- Nada Najeeb Kalappadan - 11A1

31. Childhood

I remember a decade ago,

The times when I was too young to know,

The freedom of that tender age,

Was only on a single page.

Who knew so fast we would grow,

And miss the comfort of our soft pillow?

Watch how our carefree life fades,

Into the petrifying ocean's waves.

Life is much harder now unlike the former times,

When we were jolly and unaware of the frightful crimes,

That has affected this innocent world,

Oh, how the reality starts to unfold!

And remember my friends, to enjoy your childhood to the fullest,

Engage in what you love and give it your best!

Because once we grow up, we could never know,

If we would ever get the chance for our passion to grow.

- Suaad Galal Amin - 11A2

32. The Ending

'I'm all too afraid that one day soon,
It'll become just like the rest.
Only walking with the crowd, because my steps have been
oppressed,
Like a book with torn-out pages, forgetting things you are sure
you knew.
A question with no answer, For there are missing pieces of the
puzzles.
For those who leave us for a while, Have only gone away.
Out of a restless,
careworn world.
It's the Ending that haunts me,
The simple memories completely faded.
All it takes is for this world to conquer.
Until then, it's the Ending that keeps me, levitated...

- Aishwarya Janarthany - 11A5

33. Life

Loads of memories
We had, have and will have
Enjoying every moment
That is what it is all about
Family and friends
All together,
Makes our life happy
And even easier
Happy or sad
Is all a part of life,
People must learn
Not to behave like a knife
Together gives us happiness,
Being alone leads to loneliness
Mingle with everyone kindly and smartly
This is a sign of a genius
Mixing ourselves in poisonous gangs
And following a crooked path
Is not the way of living life
For people with faith in their heart
Problems do come across
Facing them is called courage,

I hope that people understand
Suicide is for no age
Loads of memories
We had, have and will have
Enjoying every moment
That is what it is all about!!!

- Asfia Jahan Sulthana - 11A4

34. Piled up against the wall

In a trunk, brown colour
Stood the mighty pile of my books,
Untouched for a year
To give it to a mate
Oh god! I ask, what's its fate?
Its scented pages and
Smooth surfaces
Who long await to be turned
Oh god! I ask, how long does it have to wait?
To be revisited by a student ,
Eagerly, waiting to crack open
And learn and share
The light which lies behind those printed lines
Which do not die when shared, O reader
But dies when not absorbed
Oh god! I ask once again, when will that day come?
Perhaps next year,
I fear
For that's not far neither is it near,
I long to see it in someone's hand,

But utilized properly wherever
It might land
But let's think now,
Coated with dust, feather and sand,
It sits alike on the stand
Keeping me to wait for to see it in,
Someone's hand.

– Naila Siddiqui – 11A6

Chapter 35

Some might say it's bravery
Some might say that's sheer cowardness,
Others might tag as intelligent,
But little do the outsiders know what is gone
and felt.
For once done a mistake is alright,
unless repeated again
Where the latter hasn't been committed,
Yet the sufferer has to either,
retain or fight.
Amidst the cool breezy mornings
to the pleasant afternoons,
Surely comes a night with curious stars
and a full bright moon.
This world where
words as arrows, once leave the bow
Can never be taken back,
Hidden or shown.
So, when you are down heavily, and you want
to die,
Peacefully, now and alone,
Sit back and write,

All that you have gone.

- *Naila Siddiqui - 11A6*

36. Independence Struggle

In woods as dark as night,
There glistened a Sungold nest.
Its birds served as a Ray of light; To the woods so calm and
blessed.
Like every story it too had villains, Which judged the others by
colour, It was a white flock of
pigeons, Rude they were; also cold and bitter.
Jealous of the nest and its birds, They decided to colonize it.
And so befriended some of the golden birds,
To implement the evil plan they had slyly knit.
Few of the golden birdies,
Had fallen because of greed,
They had accepted the hidden jeopardies,
For power; blinded by caste and creed.
They did capture it, sadly.
But not for too long.
For the birds it was too much, frankly
"How can we let those Firangis rule us?"
Quite right they were to think it wrong.
They fought very fiercely.
For freedom. peace and equality. They had to anyhow end this,
The harsh inequality and brutality.

They belong to the nest called Bharat.
A country of diverse cultures and traditions,
And enrich beauty along with a piece of Jannat.
A place where one can only find affection.
It's my India. A place which I call my Utopia.

- Isra Abrar - 11A4

37. My Way to Heaven

I was born Innocent,
I have grown a burden, I thought to change this problem,
But it just became Random,
Tired of Being the victim,
Tired of Singing my false Anthem,
I decided to change,
And I became my new page.
I start to breathe my new air, Running around to feel the breeze
hit my hair,
And I realised my life is Euphoria, Exactly the wish I had
internally, Now noticed that my life is
short And have to spend some were eternal,
And that's when I closed my eyes with a smile,
Ready to make my way to Heaven.

- Karen - 11A3

38. That World

I desire to go to that world,
Where you will be on standby
For me,
With all the happiness.
I desire to go to that world,
Whereby no love story
will be deficient.
I desire to do to that world,
Where there is full of happiness,
And the sky was full of red.
I desire to go to that world,
Where there will be
No unsecured with anyone
Or anything.
I desire to go to that world,
Where all the girls
Will be shielded and can
Abondance safely without fear.
I desire to go to that world,
That wonderful world,
That world of gold
Where I will talk with no words.

- Fathima Miraj - 11A2

• 54 •

39. When Home feels like Hell

When nothing feels alright,
When your day is not bright,
When your body feels deadly,
When you are not able to cry.
When you have sleepless nights,
And touches don't feel alright,
When the home is another name for prison,
A nd every day you drink poison.
In bright light, you suffer,
And at night you surrender,
When your soul is just tired,
And everything in life is just blurred.
When you are trying to escape from this hell,
But it's a trap in me,
When everyday I wake up,
I hope that it will get better
But every day it's hell.

- Fathima Miraj - 11A2

40. A World, no one knows

Its when you are in a cage,
But you don't tend to change the page,
It's like I have created my blackhole
Consuming all my energy and my soul.
When you feel pins and needles on the skin,
When you realize there's no win within,
When you want to break the cage,
But you are not in the early stage.
When every opportunity is waiting for you,
When he is also waiting for you,
When you are starving in a gathering,
And you are just wandering.
When staring at dark walls feel peaceful,
But in reality, it's awful,
Yeah, you get it right
It's ANXIETY.

- Fathima Miraj - 11A2

41. The Truth Inside

this world may have peace,
but I see conflict inside.
these rooms may be crowded,
but I see lonely souls inside.
this night may be full of stars,
but I see it dark in real life.
this heart may seem healed,
but I see scars inside.
this smile may be big,
but I see lost hope inside.
these relationships may seem true,
but I see a void inside.
these roses may be beautiful,
but I see thorns in real life.
this trust may be faithful,
but I see the fear inside.
this youth may be bright,
but I see drained hearts inside.
there may be happy pictures,
but I see sorrowful stories inside.
this will may be there,
but I see no courage inside.

this bond may exist,
but I see no forever inside.
this light may be the power,
but I see it emitting energy inside.
their ambitions may be decided,
but I see no effort inside.
it may be warm outside,
but I feel cold inside.
this world may be real,
but it's an illusion in real life.

- Syeda Mahreen - 12A5

42. Friendship

I am certain that when you hear the word "friendship"
to memory lane, you will take a trip.
Friendship is a relationship,
a bond that deepens in every situation.
midship isn't something you can buy or sell,
rather a feeling that you know this person very well
Friendship is a connection between his heart,
one that cannot be severed or broken apart
At times you may fight,
but that will annoy you day and night.
These lights will cause a rift Creating a burden only your friend
can lift.
At your darkest hours,
during the ranging storm & the heavy showers.
your friend will be there to get you through,
and that is a sign of a friendship so true.
And that is when you realise,
that your friend is as special as a 1000 fireflies,
if your friend helps you when times are worse,
thenI then you share a friendship which can not be found hill
the ends of the universe

- Safaa Khatri - 12A2

43. I am Adivasi

I can hear your Whispers when I walk,
I can hear your giggles when I talk,
You find it funny, that I don't have money
Yet there once was a time when I owned avast land,
Where like my, forefather, I used to work with my own bare
hands. Those were the times I was surrounded by trees,
and everywhere I went there was a gust of cool breeze.
Then one dark night,
We were surrounded by auto machines & light
out Come a Man,
who hold ve to evacuate for the government had an Industry
plan.
Some sold their land unknowingly, others when told about job
offers sold them readily.
Those who didn't sell theirs were offered cash,
but when we denied tHey threatened and beat us & burned our
crops to ashe
In the end, we had no choice,
their pollies held more merit than our voice.
We soon became a part of the bustling city
Isolated from the world that heated us like an unwanted
committee

Those memories are still fresh in my mind,
I don't know & why they call us manKIND.
Now you know my magic story,
the story of my people to whom you are all an adivasi.

- Safaa Khatri - 12A2

44. Peace

"What is Peace?"
A question I sometimes ponder
as I walk down the sheets,
in the cities of wonder.
We must complete two levels, to attain this tranquillity, Peace of
the heart by soul
whilst expulsion of evil,
and peace of the neighbourhood community,
Spending time with loved ones,
Or reading, cooking other leisures.
Grazing on stars or walking under the sun,
anything that relaxes your soul & gives you pleasure.
The next level is all about giving, your time, money, efforts, and
love Giving to the world and not hesitating,
with good intentions is what matters all above.
But alas, how cruel this world is,
where give and take is the norm & religion.
A world of peace and quiet exists, but in one's thoughts and
imagination
However, it's not too late to plea, because not everything is blue.
We can still make it
into reality because change starts with you.

- Safaa Khatri - 12A2

• 64 •

45. The Days

Our day starts with coffee, theirs starts with cries.
They beg paradon for mercy while you ask for fries.
You play shooting games for fun,
they do all they can to save their lives and run.
Dont you understand what I am talking about?
They live on earth as if it was all a compassion drought.
The children of Syria and Palestine,
who shed blood and tears while we ask for shine.
Tell me if you think this is fair,
they aren't even getting the humanity of their share.
They are tortured and killed for power,
While the warlords sit in the tower.
The fight is for revenge or governance,
not a single thought about the mental resultant.
Violence is the last hope for the incompetent,
they pursue it and call it upliftment.
And when the weak lift a rock for shelter
They fire on it and call it terror
Oh lord! Save us from this human error
We all have a role to play, a basic human right to display.
Stand against the injustice they prepare,
whether it be by donation or just a clicked share.

Join hands to help, not just for prayer
They need our support, not just the word care
Run for th eir rescue with love in mind,
and watch all the peace and harmony come running behind.

- Sadia Noor - 12A4

46. Road Through Borders

The young boy gazes outside the car window,
Sharp mountains, vibrant trees all lined up in the meadow,
tumbled glittering sunrays tumbled on the sand,
and the confident sky made everything grand.
" We are in a new nation now" declared the man driving.
That made the boy frown, thinking his father was lying.
hesitantly he said "but it's all the same."
the same black mountains, amber desert passing fast just as they
came.
This made the adults pause and laugh.
" The roads are different" said the mother on the man's behalf.
Hearing this, the boy signed, going back to his seat
God made the earth the same and humans made differences with
concrete.

- Maryam - 12A5

47. It's all in the eyes

The eight-year-old took a quick glance, a
t the bag of treats in her father's hands.
but puts up a poker face remembering the morning,
The father smiled at her bright orbs, which he failed to ignore.
In another house, a wife looks up at a mirror she views,
making sure she had covered each and every bruise.
putting up a fake smile as she greets the guests,
But looking at her dark eyes made her mother depressed.
Everyone lies. All of them have a reason.
Some hide their delight, some others treason.
but they forget what was said by the wise,
Happiness or sorrow is all in the eyes.

- Maryam - 12A5

48. The Better Place

Lying on her death bed,
she looks at her daughter's eyes.
with an expression quite unread,
turning her weak body as she cries.
will the lord accept me?
she utters with her trembling lips.
the daughter nods as in guarantee,
still thinking things she couldn't fix.
the father embraces his daughter,
the timing surely did not allow.
she weeps hearing the people's chatter,
they say she's in a better place

- Maryam - 12A5

49. Peace

Scattered remains of a bloody night,
as far as the intensity of one's sight.
the burdened ground, dotted with bullet shells,
all these together still seem to ring victory bells.
They declared "we have won! "
but celebrating I see none.
some have lost their child, some their love,
the triumph doesn't seem to light there stove.
But same can be achieved without a touch
can yet walk together, without some holding a crutch.
letting pacifism make the appeals
passive but powerful, it's the sword that heals.
Freedom earned avoiding being beatened,
of who's resul t and liberty surely get sweetened.
let's not lose more than we gain,
let's not bygone those who were to reign.

- Maryam - 12A5

50. Not Yet

It's hard and too much for one to deal,
thinking of nothing but to sweat.
but better than frustration it is to feel,
that you will not give up, not yet.
loading the last of the magazines,
being aware of each and every threat.
still fights back ignoring the spleems,
that he will not give up, not yet.
life is not meant for one to relax,
it's not work that you'll not regret.
let will melt the worry like fire melts wax,
please it 's not over, not yet.

- Maryam - 12A5

51. The Day I Laughed Through Tears

I've seen smiles of all kinds,
But none broke out after they faced fears.
And I hope that one day, some time,
would be the day I laughed through tears.
Satisfied, breathy laughs,
after long nights of stressful prayer.
made for the perfect photographs,
would be the day I laughed through tears.
Free from judgement and stares,
After years of worry and despair.
Crowns thrown in the air with no care,
Would be the day I laughed through tears.
Another step for me.
Grander, higher,
Something worth a degree,
not a discarded flyer,
I will laugh,
I will smile,
uncaring of torn papers in half,
as I've surpassed my trial

My parents will smile with glee,
my friends would cheer,
with boisterous laughs surrounding me,
would be the day I laughed through tears.

- *Emaan Basharat Ali Khan - 12A4*

52. Reflect to Shine

I wonder what happens to all the dead wildlife,

Do they just stay to pollute the green life?

I was wrong. I figured it out. Not shy

I share with you today what they defy all the limits of the great sky.

Lying down on the ground, they move underground,

New lives step on them as they move around.

The temperature rises as hot as the sun,

The pressure binds them just like a bun.

They stay just like that for tons or millions,

But when it's the right time for them, they come out shining diamonds.

Just like them is our struggle in life,

as bright as If we can face the pressure and heat, we will no doubt survive.

Survive is not the right word, I think.

But it shines like a diamond on the very first blink.

Challenges are what make life interesting.

- Sadia Noor - 12A4

53. People

Hope, laughs, peace, happiness. Everything was shattered
When a girl, a child was born to this ancestor
Not a year that lady didn't weep
She was being fried from inside so deep…
It was a choice of god. What was her mistake?
No, it's not over yet!
Now the child has to bear some torture too.
It's a tradition that girls have to go side by side too.
Whom she considered sweetest, turned out to be venomous
Childhood, which was desired to spend with joy
Was replaced with outrageous.
Truth, facts, insults, shame punched her so high.
She didn't know where all the broken pieces of heart and mind
flew.
Never felt like hunting snakes
They were standing in front of my face.
Oh god save me from this place!!

- Misbah Tabasum

Asst. blue house captain - 12A6

• 76 •

54. The necklace; Those were the days...

That was back in the day... that was back in the day...
When Matilda Loisel had a beautiful physique,
and a charming face.
All she needed was a pretty dress and a sparkling necklace.
With that, she had zest, fervor, and pace.
To partake in the revelry,
Indeed, those were the days...
She was delighted by the spotlight.
and was squealing in delight.
When she went back to the poverty-stricken house, a dearth of a
rich height,
She was a bundle of nerves, covered in fright.
Now, the gratified evening no longer seemed like dynamite.
She couldn't trace the necklace around her neck or on her gown.
The husband and wife looked for it everywhere; left, right, up
and down.
But I still couldn't find it after dawn.
It was gone...
All gone...!

She not only lost that ornament but also her beautiful physique
and that charming face.
She no longer had the zest, fervor, or pace.
To partake in the revelry,
She now began to live in an attic where she always felt listless
and was overcome with fatigue.
Now, all she has is an atrocious life.
With all the misery and distress
no longer upholds the status of a mistress.
However, she was never a blissful wife.
Now, she sits next to the window and recalls all those moments
from that phase.
Indeed, those were the days!
Those were the days...

- Shahnaz Begum Mohammed - 12A5

55. The Value

When loneliness attacks
When thou sense darkness around,
When none takes a moment
You suffer from an unbearable wound.
Be mindful of the value!
The value of time
Which shouldn't be blown,
The value of fate
Which you shouldn't forfeit,
The value of hard work
Which shouldn't stand weak,
And not least,
The value of yourself
Which shouldn't be ignored.
Created is thou,
To live and succeed
To love and smile,
To care and forgive
And never to sit deserted,
This time isn't an eternity
Rise and twinkle to infinity,
So that you discover

The uniqueness of your voyage of life.

~ Fathimath Hiba - 12A6

Author of 'Shine With Hopes : Be A Diamond'

56. Peace

A void heart falling sick
Emotions on alarm,
Inverted smiles curve
Wants a need, that's peace.
Admiring the rain
Ignoring the pain,
Which gifts serenity
Though it fades.
Running behind the past
Memories jotted on rocks,
Never can be erased
So, learn and move.
Peace is near you
It is in thy spirit,
Unlock your heart
That's your intuitive eye,
You may feel harmony
Of sweet wonders around.
Taste the flavours of life
A hill of ups and downs,
Let the blossoms in you bloom
Go off the disturbing gloom,

It's time to wake up
To nourish your soul with peace.

- Fathimath Hiba - 12A6

Author of 'Shine With Hopes : Be A Diamond'

57. Worthy Dual

Reminding you worthy dual
Praise and purpose of life,
Like the twins of nature
The day and the night.
Give a glance
And you see one quality,
Like the unique star
Which accompanies the moon
Stare at it for long
And you see countless quantities,
Like the unending stars
In the dark deep sky.
So are the virtues of human
Stare or peep,
the Choice is yours
To acknowledge the world around you
And be grateful!
Praises ain't enough decent
When life is void,
Have a gaze at the birds
And their efforts.

Beneath the gleam shades
Gathered pieces of love,
Chitter of birds fades
Shaping a beautiful nest, wow!
Hiring the harmony gleam
The span of prolonged weeks,
Which etched into a flawless home
With tolerance and toils.
Compile your clashes like them
For, charm arrives with calm,
As twilight is admired
Over the oversight of the future.
Clutch onto it
Strives may fail,
Distance of your attempts
Describes your expert and decors of your spirit.

- Fathimath Hiba - 12A6

Author of 'Shine With Hopes : Be A Diamond'

58. The Peaceful Day

Soon after a sound sleep,
I was hoping against hope.
I expected a calm and peaceful day.
after a long, tiring Friday.
Before I had changed and after having his brunch arranged,
I went to check on my dog and found something strange.
I saw the broken straps and happened to know that Bruno had
disappeared.
I got scared and panicked as it was the only dog I had reared.
I was dragged out of my house in my nightgown;
which made me look no less than a funny circus clown.
People gav e me a look that told me I'm not supposed to wear
that while I jog,
but I cared not as I cared more about my little pet dog.
I finally spotted Bruno in a park.
I was sitting beside a man who wore all dark.
I knew that he was a criminal.
So I decided to go for a run with my dog.
I held the rope and ran as fast as I could.
And behind me ran the man in the black hood.
But I felt something very strange.
as Bruno continuously barked and became mad with rage.

I ignored it and ran faster till I reached my house, where I was
safe.
But we were all shocked to see Bruno in there, and it felt so
much like a louse!
Startled, I turned to see the dog behind me.
who wasn't as pleased as I thought he'd be.
After that, all it took was a knock on the door.
and thought there couldn't be anything more bad.
Hours later, I opened the door.
I was in jail trying hard to snore.
I now don't want any more peaceful days.
as I just had one.

— Shaikh Rukaiya - 12A6

REFLECTING THE AUTHORS

Misbah Tabasum

Asst. Blue House
Captain 2021-2022

Bharvi A. Hirvania

Asst. Literary Secretary
2021-2022 & Red
House Captain 2022-23

The intellectuals and code generators behind the entire book are **Misbah Tabasum** (Assistant Blue House Captain 2021-2022), **Bharvi A. Hirvania** (Assistant Literary Secretary 2021-2022 & Red House Captain 2022-23), **Shazia Hakeem** (Assistant Head Girl 2021-2022 & Blue House Captain 2022-23), and **Wania Kaleem Alam** (Asst. Yellow House Captain 2021-22 & Green House Captain 2022-23).

Saudi Arabia based International Indian School, Jeddah (IISJ). Student Cabinet and the student body have indeed made a significant contribution towards empowering and positively influencing the lives of countless individuals.

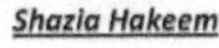

Shazia Hakeem

Asst. Head Girl 2021-
2022 & Blue House
Captain 2022-23

Wania Kaleem Alam

Asst. Yellow House
Captain 2021-22 & Green
House Captain 2022-23